**Table of Contents**

**Anatomy of Anxiety**
New Research on Anxiety and Stress Related Problems
What Doctors Don't Want You to Know
©2012 Dr. Harry Jay

# DISCLAIMER AND TERMS OF USE AGREEMENT:

**(Please Read This Before Using This Book)**
This information is for educational and informational purposes only. The content is not intended to be a substitute for any professional advice, diagnosis, or treatment.

The authors and publisher of this book and the accompanying materials have used their best efforts in preparing this book.

The authors and publisher make no representation or warranties with respect to the accuracy, applicability, fitness, or completeness of the contents of this book. The information contained in this book is strictly for educational purposes. Therefore, if you wish to apply ideas contained in this book, you are taking full responsibility for your actions.

The authors and publisher disclaim any warranties (express or implied), merchantability, or fitness for any particular purpose. The author and publisher shall in no event be held liable to any party for any direct, indirect, punitive, special, incidental or other consequential damages arising directly or indirectly from any use of this material, which is provided "as is", and without warranties. As always, the advice of a competent legal, tax, accounting, medical or other professional should be sought where applicable.

The authors and publisher do not warrant the performance, effectiveness or applicability of any sites listed or linked to in this book. All links are for information purposes only and are not warranted for content, accuracy or any other implied or explicit purpose. No part of this may be copied, or changed in any format, or used in any way other than what is outlined within this course under any circumstances. Violators will be prosecuted.

# Introduction

What I am about to introduce to you is a subject that can be easily misunderstood. And I will show you just how easy things can be misunderstood.

I am not attempting to start a cult; I am not asking anyone to drink the Kool-Aid, but I am asking you to open your minds and see things from a different perspective.

I am also not asking people to take their medical needs into their own hands and ignore competent medical advice. I firmly believe that people have definitive medical needs that a medical professional can and should address.

Most people will experience anxiety in their lifetime. Without understanding truly what anxiety and stress really are, people are suffering from problems they know little about.

So first, let's define anxiety. Anxiety is a general term used for nervousness, fear, apprehension or worry associated with uncertain outcomes.  In other words, anxiety is fear over what MAY happen either real or perceived.

Examples are panic disorders, OCD, PTSD, phobias, etc.
    Here are some eye-opening statistics:

- One out of seven Americans, ages 18 and above, is said to suffer from an anxiety disorder.  This is close to 42-million Americans or almost 19% of our population.

- Anxiety disorders are the number 1 mental health problem among women and the number 2 mental health problem among men.

- Women are twice as likely to suffer from anxiety as men.

Is there a reasonable solution?  Yes, however, as I have said in the past, as a whole people like a diagnosis more than they like the solution.  Because a diagnosis allows us to make excuses for what our lives have become and a solution challenges us to take steps for what our lives could be.  In other words, it allows us to become victims of something other than ourselves and today our country is made up almost exclusively of victims.

So is the solution as simple as focus?  Is what our minds focus on the underlying cause of anxiety and stress? Let's see…

There are thousands of experts and just as many critics

involved in the field of anxiety and stress. But all of them generally agree on four areas of viewpoint when it comes to anxiety and stress:

- Rooting around in your past experiences, primarily in your childhood, will reveal areas of problems and tension that lead to the anxiety you are suffering from today. And for $120 per hour, several times per week, for a number of years, they will be happy to play 20-questions with you.

- Others claim that the problem is environmental. If you remove the person from that particular environment then the problem is solved.

- Some even suggest that the problem can be traced back to a chemical imbalance in the brain causing the neurons to misfire and hence…anxiety.

- People focus on the wrong thoughts rather than thinking through positive thoughts. If you replace the negative with the positive than the power of positive thinking is enough to solve the problem.

Forgive me, but not only because I am a scientist, but a rational thinking human being, the cynical side of me asks, "Why is all of this happening now?" In other words, is this a generational issue, is this an American issue, is this a human issue? Let's pull back for a moment and frame this in a context that is much bigger.

Is this a human problem or is this a relatively new problem? If it is a human problem, then it should be seen in every generation, in every people group worldwide.

My take on this is simple: anxiety here in America is about a fifty year phenomena within this culture and not humanity as a whole. From 1910 to 1950 our grandparents and parents experience two world wars and the Great Depression. If any one group had a better claim to depression, anxiety and stress it would be our parents and grandparents. They should have been the most messed up generation closest to our generation. But they came home and started businesses, saved money, put their kids through college, and built America into the world power it is today. And they did all this before prescription drugs dealt with the subject of anxiety and stress!

Nobody told them to go back and look into their childhood to find their issues. So once again is this a human problem or generational problem?

How does money factor in this? On third...ONE THIRD...of the $148 billion dollars spent annually on mental health is eaten up dealing with anxiety disorders. So, before we accept all of the current research on anxiety disorders, we need to go back and ask who paid for this research.

Bottom line: ANXIETY IS BIG BUSINESS AND SOMEONE IS GETTING PAID AND SOMEONE IS GETTING PAID REAL WELL!

And I am not alone in my skepticism either. There are thousands of doctors sounding the alarm saying watch out because the medication given to people to treat anxiety disorders is doing irreparable harm

Dr. Peter Breggin in his book "Brain Disabling Treatments in Psychiatry" said, "At present, there are no known bio-chemical imbalances in the brain of typical psychiatric patients until they are given psychiatric drugs."

Dr. Eric Nestler of Yale University School of Medicine, "Psychiatric drugs are like sledgehammers; they profoundly alter many of the pathways in our brain."

Dr. Lorrin Koran states, "A physical disease that is incorrectly diagnosed as a mental disorder can lead to a lifetime on psycho-tropic drugs, loss of productivity, physical and social deterioration and shattered dreams."

Dr. David Kaiser points out, "Patients have been diagnosed with chemical imbalances despite the fact that no test exists to support such a claim."

Now let's delve deeper into the subject and learn about the core foundation of what doctors use to treat anxiety disorders.

# Chapter 1 - Defining Psychology

The word "psychology" is the combination of two terms - study (ology) and soul (psyche), or mind. The derivation of the word from Latin gives it this clear and obvious meaning:

The study of the soul or mind!

This meaning has been altered over the years until today this is not what the word means at all. The subject of psychology, as studied in colleges and universities, currently has very little to do with the mind, and absolutely nothing to do with the soul or spirit.

It is important to understand that words and ideas are supposed to refer to something. "The large tree in the front yard" refers to an actual thing that can be seen, touched and experienced. "The man walking his little dog last night at sunset" refers to an actual event that can be seen, observed and experienced. The realm of mind is an actual realm that can be experienced, and at one time there were words that accurately referred to this realm.

Let's see what a few dictionaries have to say and how a word could alter and lose its true and actual meaning.

"Psyche" is defined as:

1. The spirit or soul.

2. The human mind.

3. In psychoanalysis, the mind functioning as the center of thought, emotion, and behavior.

And defining "soul", we have:

1. The physical manifestations of the body combined with the immortal elements in a person.
2. A person's mental or moral or emotional nature.

Most of us would agree we have a "psyche" per the above definitions in the sense of mind, thought, and emotions. Most would also agree they have a "soul" per the second definition above relating to man's mental, moral or emotional nature. We might all have different notions about what these ultimately are, but few could sanely disagree they exist.

The derivation of "psyche" comes from Latin and the Greek *psukhe* - breath, life, soul.

To get a better "feel" for this term try to think of it as the invisible animating principle or entity that occupies, interacts with and directs the physical body.

We are not dealing with opinions or beliefs here. This is simply what the words and terms mean. Get clear on this first and understand what the words and terms mean, before you start getting into the opinions of others on the subject. If you choose to decide the "mind" refers to nothing real after understanding what the words and definitions mean, despite the fact that almost 6,000 years of thinking men have seriously and carefully looked into this subject, and after no real investigation on your own part, then that's your decision.

Also, realize you will be basing this decision on "thinking" and "reason", both of which are only subsidiary to and *part* of any one mind, and neglecting to use a greater aspect of your mind - your personal awareness and direct observation.

Basing a decision on what other people say about a mind involves only *concepts* and *ideas* about a mind. Observation involves *experiencing the mind itself* - your own mind. When it comes to minds there is only one mind any of us can directly observe or experience and that mind is our own.

If you want to learn about minds, the only place to start is with your own. You cannot directly observe or experience the mind of another person, at least not without some extrasensory ability such as telepathy.

# Chapter 2 - What is the Mind?

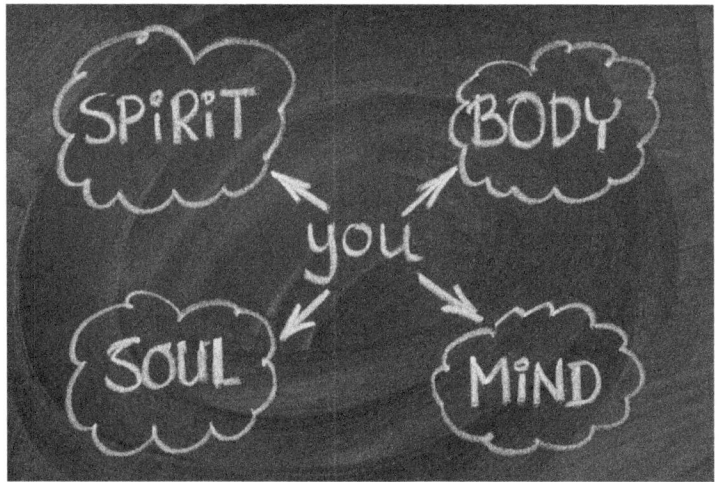

Originally, and for thousands of years, the subject of psychology involved the study of the human spirit, soul or mind. This involves things and functions not obviously visible to the physical senses. You can't see a mind with one's eyes. You can't "feel" a thought with one's hands. You can't place an emotion on a scale and weigh it. You can't detect imagination, even with sophisticated electronic detection devices. Just because some scientist's electronic device measures various electronic pulses or signals when you are asked to imagine something does not at all mean that they are "measuring imagination".

What they are measuring is some brain reaction that occurs *when* you initiate an act of imagination. There *is* a relationship between the mind and the brain, but this relationship is almost completely unknown and not understood. The same is true for any chemical reactions or events that occur concurrent with imagination, thoughts or feelings. There *is* some relationship, but it is poorly understood. In fact, the entire framework of the relationship is poorly conceived. Modern "scientific" fields, since they haven't been able to study or detect these things with the physical senses or laboratory measuring devices have taken a drastic leap and declared that these things therefore don't exist. They have therefore asserted that these things don't deserve recognition, and should be ignored in any "legitimate" study of man, the mind, and human behavior. John Watson, a typical secular behavioral psychologist had this to say:

*The extent to which most of us are shot through with a savage background is almost unbelievable.... One example of such a religious concept is that every individual has a* soul *which is separate and distinct from the body.... No one has ever touched a soul, or seen one in a test tube, or has in any way come into relationship with it as he has with the other objects of his daily experience...*

*The secular behaviorist asks: Why don't we make what we can* observe *the real field of psychology? Let us limit ourselves to things that can be observed, and formulate laws concerning only those things. Now what can we observe? We can observe* behavior - *what the organism does or says. And let us point out at once: that* saying *is doing - that is,* behaving . . . - John Watson, behaviorist

**Strangely, the study of the mind has come into the peculiar position of being a study that denies the mind! That's like biology denying the existence of biological organisms, but going on pretending to still be the science of biological organisms while actually dealing with something else entirely. A subject can't exist if it denies the very basis of its own existence by definition. That is the state of modern western psychology and psychiatry. Mmmm? They can't and shouldn't exist, but they do. The entire structure of these subjects as they currently exist is a sham.**

Let's take a closer look at this. We each are quite aware we have a mind, emotions, and thoughts, even if we are not so clear or sure about the "soul" and "spirit". We know we are aware and possess self-awareness, but what the nature, qualities and potentials are of awareness is largely anybody's guess.

We each know we possess consciousness. In fact, we are aware of our own consciousness as much or more than anything else, yet modern "science" ignores and even denies it. But the truth, despite what "science" or "professionals" say, is that the mind exists to and for each of us as an obvious and observable fact of direct experience. A quick look can tell us many obvious things.

I doubt any of us would suggest we don't have a mind, awareness, thoughts or feelings even though none of these things can be detected or perceived with the

15

physical senses or "scientific" measuring gadgets. No third party observer can directly observe or detect *any* of these things. *We don't immediately run off and deny their existence* and we correctly assume others have similar minds, thoughts, feelings and emotions. They do. Modern psychologists and psychiatrists, for all practical purposes, completely deny every aspect of the invisible world known to you as your mind. It *is* invisible to physical detection, but it *does* exist. In fact, it very much exists, but it is not made up of anything physical. While the mind deals with and relates to some subtle forms of energy, in the end it cannot be understood within the framework of matter or energy. Of course, any card-carrying materialist naturally hates that idea with a passion. To them, "if I can't measure it then it doesn't exist".

There is constant activity within each of our "invisible worlds". We are each in some way constantly analyzing problems, entertaining thoughts of tomorrow's occurrences, recalling yesterday's failures, wallowing in the sadness of a loss, concentrating on the creation of a musical composition, or day-dreaming. There are ever changing feelings and emotions about everything we experience, and an endless parade of judgments and commentary about what we see. Actually, for many of us, we have *too much* mind. It goes on and on and never seems to stop. It is a constant source of images, memories and ideas intruding themselves upon our awareness. Most of us can't control any of this and simply accept as inevitable this continual parade of images and ideas appearing across the landscape of our mind.

**In a very real manner *all problems* with any mind, such as things psychiatry calls "depression", "anxiety", "compulsive disorder", "Attention Deficit Disorder" (ADD or ADHD), and even "suicidal ideation", are ultimately and solely *uncontrollable aspects of one's own mind that intrude upon the person's awareness*. It's not that these things don't exist in some way, but they don't exist in the way psychiatry understands and claims to solve them. A better way to handle these problems would be to assist the person to *increase control over the content of their own mind*. There are many ways to do this, although they have never been all pulled together, adequately investigated, codified and organized into a straight-forward workable compilation of methods. Modern "science" has simply discarded the notion of the mind, and from that point on, never bothered to investigate it closely with the aim to understand, solve or improve it.**

First, this invisible world *is* totally real. It is *not* imaginary or a hallucination. My invisible world isn't directly real to you, and your invisible world isn't directly real to me, but they are *each real nonetheless*. The person who wants to argue this fact is simply a fool, dull, unable to comfortably observe his *own* mind (because it is possibly filled with degraded and nasty things), and probably addicted to the objects of physical sensation and perception to the exclusion of anything else (a modern materialist).

Second, this "invisible" world of mind involves many different aspects, functions and potentials. Imaginations, attention, intellect, awareness, intention, reason, will, responsibility, memory, and many other things exist in each of us. They are a vital and important part of us. Some people might venture to say some of these things ARE us. There is much to each of these areas and a short attempt to articulate them cannot begin to even scratch the surface of their nature, functioning, possible development and capabilities. But they definitely *do exist* and deserve recognition and attention. Any subject calling itself "psychology" would have to address *these things* in detail. The failure of modern psychology and psychiatry to do so is glaringly apparent. These subjects now only address behavior, physiology, genetics and biochemistry, and the mind is of no real concern. *That* is a very sad comment on the current state of "modern psychology".

# Chapter 3 - Psychology Definition Altered

Let's return now to the dictionary definitions of "psychology".

From the *Oxford American Dictionary*:

1. The study of the mind and how it works.
2. Mental characteristics, *can you understand his psychology?*

That's fine.

From the *Concise Oxford Dictionary*:

1. The scientific study of the human mind and its functions, esp. those affecting behavior in a given context.
2. A treatise on or theory of this.
3. the mental characteristics or attitude of a person or group
4. the mental factors governing a situation or activity (*the psychology of crime*)

Definition 1 has slyly added the idea of "affecting behavior". The original definition had nothing to do with this. The wish to control the minds and actions of others has entered into the equation.

From the *American Heritage Dictionary*:

1. The science that deals with mental processes and behavior.
2. The emotional and behavioral characteristics of an individual or group.

These definitions have further altered the true meaning. In actual practice, modern psychology deals almost exclusively with physiology (brain chemistry, neurology, genetics) and the behavior of the biological organism (stimulus-response), completely disregarding and ignoring the mind (man's inner self, and more to the point, man's true and vital self). The dictionaries will sooner or later remove the concept of "mind" completely from the definition following the lead of "official" psychology as taught in western universities and colleges.

Members of the educational establishment write the dictionaries, and the educational establishment is entrenched in modern psychological theories. Let's return to the correct definition of the word.

**Adhering to the strict definition of the word, psychology would involve the study of man's invisible world as described above, and nothing else. By definition this is what the study would deal with. This is not an opinion or bias. This is according to exactly what the word means and nothing else. Of course, relations to behavior could be studied, and relations to brain activity could be studied, but the subject in itself, by definition is or should be the study of the mind or soul. A more correct name for the modern subjects of psychology and psychiatry would be "people control" because that's what they actually are. They are subjects involving how to alter thoughts, attitudes and behavior. The intention is to control people. That in a nutshell is the purpose of behaviorism. Naturally governments and totalitarians love the subject. They also fund it in large way.**

# Chapter 4 - A Legitimate Study of the Mind

What would a study of the mind entail? It would investigate the nature, functioning, and potentials of man's inner and invisible mental activity. This would encompass such things as awareness, attention, intention, imagination and concentration. It would develop techniques for any individual to first, become aware of these functions, and to also strengthen and expand their use and control of these functions. It would also investigate the *actual source* of the problems anyone experiences with their own mind. Again, these things do exist, can be observed by anyone caring to examine *their own mind*, and involve a tremendous uncharted area of possible exploration, investigation, codification and summarizing.

Freudian psychology and psychotherapy, despite all its faults, at least recognized and partially examined this realm. For a subject calling itself the "science of the mind" to omit all this is a huge failure of modern psychology. It's actually absurd and would be laughable if the results of what they do weren't so insidious. It is equally laughable that many of these overly-educated boobs talk together as if they are the absolute pinnacle of truth about the subject of psychology. Sadly, too many others accept their claims and treat them as if they actually deserve respect, support and admiration. They don't.

This has nothing to do with mysticism, spiritualism (communicating with the dead), astral travel, OBE (out-of-body experiences), or psychic phenomena. It's not that these don't or can't exist, but a serious and scientific examination of the mind need not involve or explain these things.

**It might eventually, but it isn't necessary. The point is you *do have a mind*. It is more *you* than anything else. You can take away your possessions, your family, your friends, your job, your arms, your legs, your torso, your ears, your nose, your jaw, your skull, and the one thing that remains, which always remains, and which is closest to your basic identity, is your *mind*. This is the invisible space and activity you are aware of every second of every day and that most people experience as existing "in their head". This realm has been grossly ignored by modern psychological studies and theories to our continual detriment and harm.**

Some of this may be hard for some readers to understand or accept because an actual study and involvement with the mind isn't done at all under the current subject of psychology. It's strangely absent from most modern concepts of Man. This concept has been largely eradicated from the "modern world view".

**Notions of the mind and related ideas about it have been falsely equated to "religion," "spiritualism," or "mysticism". We each have a mind. You know it, and I know it. We each experience it and its many various aspects as mentioned above. This is very simple and straightforward.**

Modern psychology, due to absurd notions, flawed presumptions, intellectual dullness, observational weakness, blatant prejudice, and tremendous financial concerns ignores the mind completely, and *instead* concentrates on physiology, and analyzing and controlling animal behavior and responses to environmental factors. It's not that you don't have a body and use it to play your part in life. You do. There *is* physiology, and the environment *does* affect each and every one of us. But the current subject *pretends* to be a study of the mind and Man, and having failed completely at that has abandoned and finally denied the very existence of Man's mind. Worse, it pretends to be the *final word on the subject*, all the while attacking and suppressing any honest study or subject that deals with the actual field of the mind.

**Evolutionists do not appear to see the difference between the matter part of an organism and the life part, which animates it. They seem to think that the organism itself is life. Psychology suffers a similar problem of understanding.**

Modern psychology and psychiatry claim validity by posturing as "science". They claim to "study Man as an object of investigative science". They fail at this because any *legitimate* science should and would take into account *all* aspects of the subject it deals with. A valid science would not choose to omit a major body of data from its analysis, which is what they have done with the mind.

Dealing with, examining, and limiting observations to a specific *smaller* realm of data, while ignoring a very large area of other data, which it finds inconvenient because it fails to conform to their pet theories, is exactly what has been done by the modern fields of psychology and psychiatry. Failing to take the *entire* subject matter into account has resulted in incorrect theories, faulty observations, flawed basic assumptions, and unworkable results.

Considering that every decent, creative, and wonderful thing in existence in the physical world started as an *idea* in the invisible and unobservable *mind* of someone should make this denial of the mind by "modern science" a major cause for alarm. This is doubly true when one also considers that every problem in society largely has its source in actual problems with an individual mind. Education and the environment may heavily influence problems with crime, violence, abuse, and sexual deviancy, but ultimately the final basic source of these problem areas resides in the individual minds of people.

# Chapter 5 - The Harmful Results of Denying the Mind

When the mind is denied, so ultimately is every good and decent thing that emanate from it including creativity, self-determinism, responsibility, morality, reason, and a value of life itself. The current decadent notion of man without a mind or inner personality, considered only as an animal or a biological organism has been institutionalized into the theories and practices of modern civilization in the media, sociology, education, government, economics, health, and of course, psychology and psychiatry.

This has had disastrous consequences in the form of increasing crime, divorce, violence, and decreasing levels of education, morality, personal responsibility, social stability and sanity. Simply, when the source of life itself for the individual and society is denied, oppressive practices parading as "science" surface and the quality of life and sanity rapidly deteriorates. This is the exact condition of modern western civilization. Psychiatric lobotomy, electric shock treatment, psychoactive drugs, behavioral manipulation, mass population control, and social development instead of intellectual education in the schools serve as a few examples.

It has become popular in modern society for people to toss off, giggle about, ridicule and flippantly criticize any alternative subject of the mind (i.e. yoga, meditation, ritual magic, Rosicrucianism, Scientology, etc.) It is *in vogue* to consider these weird and unusual. And true enough, some of them *are* weird. But the only really weird and unusual thing is that modern man is so dull and heavily indoctrinated that he is almost completely incapable of a) looking at anything fairly, b) getting involved in it more than superficially, c) examining it in some detail, d) remaining honest about what he observes and e) deciding for himself based upon accurate personal observations. This reduction in mental and observational ability is also a result of modern educational practices. These practices are direct descendants of modern psychological theories that view man as a "social organism", and tend to ignore his intellectual and cognitive abilities and development (i.e. aspects of a mind).

A leading psychological text begins by very carefully saying that today the word "psychology" does not refer to the mind or soul, and "has to be studied by its own history", since it no longer refers to the soul, or even to the mind. The *Diagnostic and Statistical Manual (DSM-IV)*, the psychiatric bible of "mental disorders" states,

*Although this volume is titled the Diagnostic and Statistical Manual of Mental Disorders, the term mental disorder unfortunately implies a distinction between "mental" disorders and "physical" disorders that is a reductionistic anachronism of mind/body dualism.*

They readily admit ignoring the "mind" as a thing of itself to be studied or understood. The current subject is spiritually bankrupt and all that emanates from it denies life, and everything positive about humanity. The logical conclusion of modern psychological theory is that man is an animal to be genetically bred, controlled, herded, and placed into suitable environments. This is the approach of the modern social planner and behavioral controller. These are the guys who governments fund, support and listen to. Is it any wonder things aren't going so well on planet Earth?

Mr. P.D. Ouspensky says it well:

**To begin with I must say that practically never in history has psychology stood at so low a level as at the present time. It has lost all touch with its origin and its meaning so that now it is even difficult to define the term "psychology": that is, to say what psychology is and what it studies. And this is so in spite of the fact that never in history has there been so many psychological theories and so many psychological writings. - The Psychology of Man's Possible Evolution, 1950**

He also adds that psychology may be the "oldest science and unfortunately, in its most essential features *a forgotten science.*" A brief look at history is in order so the reader can understand more of what a true subject of psychology might entail.

# Chapter 6 - The History of Psychology

For thousands of years psychology existed under the name of philosophy. The Hindu *Vedas* contain the oldest record of man's examination of mind and spirit. In India all forms of *Yoga*, which are essentially psychology, are described as one of the six systems of philosophy. *Sufi teachings*, which again are chiefly psychological, are regarded as partly religious and partly metaphysical. In more modern times some version of these systems, still largely following in this same vein, can be found the subjects of Rosicrucianism, New Thought, Science of Mind, visualization techniques, practical magic, and Scientology.

If you found yourself flinching or reacting negatively to the mention of any of these subjects, such as Yoga, Rosicrucianism, Scientology, or any of the many other alternative approaches to the mind and reality, realize this is not necessarily because there is anything actually strange or weird about these subjects. It is often largely because modern psychology, psychiatry and affiliated proponents of modern materialistic "science" have successfully applied black PR to them to such a large degree. In fact, they have covertly attacked these subjects for most of this century. An intelligent and objective look into any of these fields, although sometimes initially confusing largely due to the newness of the subject and difference in approach to reality will result in a widened understanding of yourself (and Man in general). Granted, you do need to and in fact you MUST weed out some of the nonsense often added to these subjects. Once you do take an honest look though it should become very obvious that modern western psychology has little to do with that incredible universe that exists a few inches behind your forehead. It must be mentioned that over time most of these subjects and fields (i.e. Scientology, Rosicrucianism, Transcendental Meditation, etc) have most definitely suffered from some combination of a) gross alterations introduced by self-appointed leaders following internal power struggles, b) manipulation of views and information by the more influential members, c) the sad tendency of some of the not-too-bright members to dictate changes not part of the original information, and d) the use of the subject and field to exert thought control and behavioral manipulation on its members. These faults are observably true and easily seen in the recent history of Scientology, though these faults exist in all to some degree. Lastly though, don't throw out the baby with the bathwater. While these all have serious flaws, don't use that as an excuse to dismiss everything about them outright without any serious examination. It takes careful and serious examination to separate the valuable from the invaluable - and there are often much of both to be found.

The mind *has* been examined, studied, drilled and "expanded", at times to the point of excruciating detail within many fields (i.e. Tibetan Buddhist Yogic practices). This is not to say that due to language barriers and the passage of time, that the information has not been lost to minor or major degrees or that these studies weren't without many errors, serious flaws, biases and differing opinions to start with. The point is **not** whether any of these are perfect studies (none are) or whether any of them have completed the task of researching the mind (none have), but that the *possibility for such a study most surely exists*, has been done before in various ways and to differing degrees, and that *modern psychology (and psychiatry) has **nothing** to do with this field.*

# Chapter 7 - The Fraud of Modern Psychiatry

Psychiatrists will argue and say they use "mental" criteria routinely to diagnose mental illness. They do. But we need to take a closer look at what they do.

They never observe the mind with an intention to empower or strengthen its capabilities.

This is covered in detail elsewhere.

Man and his societies cannot achieve happiness or success when the most basic and true aspect of Man has been denied and oppressed through institutionalized flawed belief systems parading as "science".

Modern psychological theories, in the form of psychiatry, genetics, behavioral science, social science, (and used by humanists and atheists to justify their positions):

> 1) are completely false omitting the key part of the subject (the mind), 2 pretend to be authoritative when they are factually not this at all, and 3) having been accepted and adopted by most major social and government institutions, directly allow the possibility and existence of the oppressive treatment of humanity. Man is viewed as nothing more than a fancy animal, and is treated as an animal.

Ken Kesey's book, and the movie starring Jack Nicholson, *One Flew Over The Cuckoo's Nest*, is not simply a social analogy portraying modern society's dislike and ultimate destruction of anyone who consistently upsets the status quo. It *is* this, but it also is exactly what the story line indicates.

It is a graphic story clearly showing the lack of humanity, oppression, coercion, brute force and destructiveness of the modern "mental health" field. Without the firm denial of Man and his mind, they're largely the same thing in the end, none of these things could ever occur.

The movie contains many situations where the status quo attempts to control those who choose to walk outside the system and force them back into line. Modern psychiatry and psychology primarily serve that function of control seemingly required by society and civilization. It is not about help and betterment. It has never been about help or betterment. It *should* be about help and betterment.

# Chapter 8 - The Errors of Modern Science and the Human Mind

Any person seriously concerned about Man, his mind, and society needs to be aware of exactly how "science" views and deals with these things. "Science" is fundamentally a method of investigation. The term "science" or "scientific" is erroneously attached to many fields of "study" that have very little to do with an honest application of the "scientific method". The majority of the "social sciences" is a misnomer. Due to the nature of Man, his mind, and of all resulting social manifestations (i.e. groups of individual human beings); a "scientific" analysis of Man is quite impossible and useless.

The "scientific method" has been most successful with the hard physical sciences, such as physics, chemistry, electronics and engineering (applied physical science). In each of these the scientists observe phenomena, develop theories, construct test, conduct tests, observe test results, alter the theories as necessary, re-test, and continue this until they can achieve the same results consistently. The goal is complete, one-hundred percent repeatability and consistency. This enables exact predictability and complete control of results. Thus, bridges stay up, radios tune into stations day after day, rockets fire and move the payload up into space, and so on. Most of what we enjoy in modern life is the result of direct applications of science in the realm of physics, chemistry or electronics.

**Calling something "science" or trying to apply the scientific method to situations where total consistency and predictability are not possible is ludicrous. This is the case with people and society, with the subjects of psychology, psychiatry, and sociology. Additionally, the goal of the application of the scientific method in the raw sciences is complete, total control of the environment and results. That is the nature of the application of the scientific method in the pure sciences (and engineering). The desired aim is *control*. The aim is total control.**

This concept is unworkable for human beings. The notion of controlling the environment and human society to complete and total predictability can only degrade to totalitarianism.

There is no sane, decent or empowering method possible for "social engineering". The idea is actually absurd.

What *is* needed with people is empowering them with education, increasing mental ability, and expanding the powers of their individual intelligence.

You can put two people in the same exact environment and they will "react" or respond two different ways. The idea of establishing exact environments (i.e. experimental test conditions) and obtaining one-hundred percent consistent results with human beings from one to the next is ridiculous. It is a completely dumb notion.

"Science" as traditionally applied to the physical universe is useless when applied to human beings and their societies in the same way, with the aim to total predictability and control. In fact, it's worse than useless; it's very harmful to Man and his societies. It's not only that it can't work, but results are produced that are *worse* than if they did nothing at all.

The goal of science as applied to the physical sciences is incompatible with human beings and his or her societies. "Science" *per se* cannot be successfully applied in any traditional way that empowers, helps or assists Man to rise to higher states and conditions of existence.

"Science" can and has been applied to the physical environment to improve conditions benefiting Man's physical survival, but that is not at all the same as applying "science" to Man, his mind, and his societies.

Few recognize this distinction. It is a very important and vital distinction.

The mastery gained over the environment through the physical sciences has had numerous and amazing benefits for Mankind. The same thing cannot be said for the fields of psychology, psychiatry and sociology, which claim to be "scientific" and following in the "scientific tradition". It is impossible to apply the scientific method to people and societies and obtain positive results. Look around. A few examples should suffice to show the inherent flaws of the current approach.

**Example #1:**

There is a book entitled *The Three Faces of Eve*. It is about a woman who had multiple personalities to the point where each was separate, markedly different, and unaware of what the others would think, decide, and do. At some point in the past psychiatrists and psychologists noticed this phenomena. Upon further investigation it was discovered that people with this condition, known as "Dissociative Identity Disorder" and earlier as "Multiple Personality Disorder", usually had traumatic early life experiences that acted to precipitate the condition. These were usually violent and often involved severe sexual abuse.

How does "science" handle this? "Science" wants to "learn" what "causes" it, what the various factors are, and how the various factors relate to each other and the overall condition. They want to quantify everything like all good scientists want to do. How do they do this? They are not content to study past cases. Reading stories of such cases and listening to personal anecdotes do not satisfy them. The only "scientific" way to do it is by setting up carefully planned experiments involving severe sexual abuse, violence, and personality shattering experiences, observing the "results" of these experiments, and re-testing based upon the observations of their previous testing. Of course this is grossly immoral and decadent by any standard of human decency, but these folks who demand such experiments in the "name of science" have never been known to possess the qualities of decency, compassion or morality. The same logic, moral justification and "scientific methodology" of a Dr. Mengele, Nazi medical experimenter, is alive today with these folks.

Science *has* been a success when applied to the physical realm of matter and energy. Combine two chemicals under a certain temperature and pressure and the resulting reaction is the same if conditions are kept consistent. Drop a rock with a certain mass in a vacuum and it accelerates and reaches the same terminal velocity every time. Science gains knowledge and control over matter and energy by establishing theories, conducting experiments, observing results, re-theorizing, conducting more experiments, until the results of the experiments can be duplicated consistently every time. This approach doesn't work with people and societies, although this hasn't stopped a tremendous number of deluded psychiatrists, psychologists and social scientists from trying. Even the term "social scientist" is downright absurd. It's an oxymoron. The two words cannot be put together in the same phrase and make any sense, at least not to a truly sensible person.

Continuing with our example of Eve, enter the CIA and other secretive government organizations. What purpose could a government intelligence agency have for a spy, agent or courier who could be numerous different personalities, all of which were quite unaware of what the others were thinking and doing and all of whom could be controlled by intelligence agency superiors? To the demented minds of these types of people the creation of such wonderful spies and agents would be a dream-come-true. So naturally they (probably) spent much time and money attempting to understand the mechanics of multiple personalities and creating their "perfect spy". Their excuse was "national security". The psychiatrists excuse was "gaining knowledge" and "understanding" the "true functioning of Man". Both of their excuses are nothing more than intellectual justifications for moral decadence, an utter lack of compassion and extreme harm to their fellow human beings.

They couldn't do this out in the open, because taking two to six year old children, submitting them to torture, sexual abuse, and extreme violence is not something the majority of humanity considers acceptable. Realize they wanted to "understand" completely the mechanics of the creation of multiple personality disorder, and develop the ability to successfully apply their theories and methods with *exact results*.

This is the "scientific method" applied to one phenomena of human life. They wanted to understand all the variables. They wanted to *intentionally* bring about multiple personalities, using all the means necessary, to obtain their "perfect spies". How did they do this? How are they probably now still doing this? They apply the methods of "science" to people, and experiment within the context of the subject (i.e. sexual abuse, torture, pain, degradation, etc.).

**Realize they almost never experiment in the direction of helping, improving or empowering the individual, but instead almost always experiment to bring out the most horrific and degraded of possible human qualities. They do this for "pure science", "national security", "bringing about order" and other absurd abstract notions, which make total sense to them within the context of their deluded view of reality.**

Obviously they must ensure there is absolutely no way they can be tied to what they are doing. They would need covers. They would need groups who *already* involve themselves in such activities. The following areas have probably been used as covers for such experiments:
CIA MK-Ultra mind control experiments conducted in Canada under the supervision of psychiatrist Dr. Ewen Cameron.

Black Magic Cults - Cult Ritual Abuse
Prostitution rings
Snuff films/ S & M / child pornography business
Child kidnapping & the human slave trade

The CIA would have had to make contacts and associations with very unsavory folks to carry out their plans. They did and probably still do. It would all be very "hush-hush", denied completely and they would probably do whatever they had to do to maintain their appearance of innocence and non-involvement. The utter fantastic nature of it all is their primary protection. Who would believe anyone, much less members of our own government, could or would do such things.

Black magic cults were probably infiltrated or *created*, so that severe violence, sexual abuse and emotional trauma to young children could be enacted, controlled, manipulated, and results carefully observed and recorded. Total "scientific control" would be required. Naturally these areas would also act as "recruiting pools" for their future spy resources. Cult ritual abuse *does* exist, but it exists today *much more* than it ever would have otherwise without the activities of these "intelligence" agencies and psychiatrists.

See what is actually occurring here. The psychiatrists first *create* the conditions, using the pretense of "gaining knowledge", and then come along and pretend to understand it and supply solutions to the problems they largely created in the first place, but which they deny all association with, and instead blame on "natural" and "self-existing" "mental illness" and "psychological disorders". If they had simply stayed out of it from the start the situations wouldn't exist to the degree that they do today. The same is true for violence, crime, immorality, and lone-nut assassins, who each always had undergone psychiatric treatment before committing their crime most likely in association with some covert intelligence agency psychological programmer. They will *never* "solve" these things. It is *their* theories and practices that largely *create* these things! If you believe otherwise you are as deluded as they are. If psychiatry and its influences could suddenly and magically be removed from every area of society, you would not believe the sudden change for the better in society and the improved individual "mental health" of people but back to the psychological "scientists".

To "understand" they would have had to test and *create* the conditions. They would have had to initiate very exact and controlled situations. The "scientists" would have wanted to ascertain just *how severe* an emotional shock was necessary to cause "dissociation", *how many* severe shocks were needed to create a permanent separation of a distinct "personality", how many *distinct personalities* could be created, and what type abuse was necessary to keep the personalities *operational*, separate and distinct. What type shock does the creation of dissociated personalities require?

Forced intercourse with pain and bleeding, physical abuse, torture, mutilation, sleep deprivation, food deprivation, sensory deprivation, murder of pets and even loved ones in plain sight of a young child, torture and murder of "friends" in plain sight, degrading activities such as smearing feces and urine all over their bodies, defecating on them, urinating on them, extreme verbal abuse and attacks, and on and on. Multiple personalities don't come about because a little boy loses his favorite comic book or a little girl loses her favorite doll. It takes *severe* trauma of a continuing and brutal nature. This requires abuse capable of reducing a human being to a complete animal devoid of all sense, reason, hope, love, care or any positive human qualities. It requires a complete destruction of the person's mind, emotions, and sense of self. They also discovered that for the dissociation to be most effective the initial major shocks must occur under the age of six. They probably discovered this by repetitive, continual, and intense abuse of many innocent children. "When you've got to know, you've got to know . . .". Who am I to stop the forward progress of science? (Extreme sarcasm here)

**But according to the CIA "intelligence" mentality, "we must protect our national security", and to the experimenting psychiatrists, "we must apply 100% objective science toward understanding the true nature of Man". Be sure of one thing, they submitted innocent children to horrendous treatments in their search and continuing actions to "understand the mechanics of MPD" and to maintain their "perfect" spies. They all deserve to be drawn and quartered in plain public view and I honestly pray there will be a very special place in eternal Hell for all of them! No penalty would be too severe for what they have done, regardless of their "sensible" excuses and justifications of "science" and "national security". As far as I am concerned, any group that would condone such activities doesn't deserve to be protected or maintained.**

The thing these type folks *never* seem to be capable of understanding is that Man can be so many different things. If Man is treated like a mindless animal he will tend to act like one. But if Man is treated like a thinking, capable, and responsible being, and given the tools to become such a being, he also tends to act this way. It isn't a matter of figuring out what man *actually is*, as the modern proponents of "science" claim to be doing, but more deciding what we *want him to be*. Because Man *can be anything*, from the very absolute worst to the most fantastic best! Modern psychiatry and psychology view Man as an animal, as a biological organism, as a beast to be controlled, and *not as a mind*. Viewing Man as an animal will send him further *down* in that direction. Viewing Man *as a mind*, with all that entails, will send him *up* to greater heights and possibilities and in another direction entirely.

These "scientists" want to "know" and will do just about anything to "increase their knowledge". Apparently, various intelligence organizations have worked with and through various illegal activities and organizations to conduct their experiments and continue their covert spy operations, all the while working with "brilliant" psychiatrists and social "scientists". These psychiatric "professionals" hold degrees and professorships at the best colleges and universities. They are members and leaders of influential psychiatric associations and publications. But more to the point, these people are and always have been the worse type of criminals. They have absolutely no sense of humanity or decency, despite everything they pretend and assert. They are despicable examples of humanity pretending to be something else entirely. They are most certainly not decent, honest human beings, and they will deserve completely whatever ill fate finally befalls them.

The goal of the psychiatrists, psychologists and intelligence organizations is to CONTROL human behavior. They want to be able to control human behavior just as the physical scientist controls chemicals, electronics, or metals. They want 100% consistent results all of the time. They want people to behave as they feel they should. The thing they always lose sight of is that human beings are *not* simply chemicals, electrons or energy. You can't simply push on a human being a certain way and have him keep going in the same direction, like a rock or brick on a frictionless surface. People are not simply matter and energy. Human beings are entities of *consciousness* with thought, awareness, will, attention, purposes, goals, imagination, responsibility and creativity. Human beings don't simply do what they are told. They decide and *then* act. They learn through education, personal desire and intention. Trying to force human beings into a mold conforming to the same paradigm as that which understands the physical sciences is severely flawed and has disastrous consequences for people and society. People *aren't* rocks. People *aren't* electrons running through a wire in an electric circuit. Treating them as such goes nowhere. Actually that's not quite true; it's worse; treating them as such causes individual deterioration, personal disasters and widespread social failure.

The methods and goals of science as applied to the raw physical universe of matter and energy are incompatible and unworkable in the realm of Man, his mind, and his societies. One-hundred percent total control and predictability of atoms, chemicals, and electrons is useful and works. One-hundred percent total control and predictability of people and societies is not useful and doesn't work. In fact it's a degrading and idiotic idea. But that is the trend of modern psychology, psychiatry, and sociology. These fields are filled with many powerful people, with large salaries, and with lots of letters after their names (i.e. Ph.D.) who are basically fools. In too many cases they are nasty fools.

**Example #2:**

Another example is religion. Social psychologists, sociologists, and government types noticed at some point that certain people have committed really strange and despicable crimes due to their religious or intense personal beliefs. This is very true. People have done many strange things in the name of some religion. There was obviously some relationship between the religious structure, beliefs and resultant actions. But again, simply studying past cases and depending on anecdotal evidence wouldn't be enough for them.

Sociologists, psychologists and psychiatrists wanted to "understand" and "learn" how religion can be used to *control* people. "How can we use religion and beliefs to get people to do what we want?" "How far will they go in the name of a religion?" What are the variables involved? How do these variables interact and relate? There was never any intention to ascertain whether there is any validity to the subjects of various religions.

**There is much evidence that the Jonestown mass murder, called mass suicide in the media, involving Jim Jones and the People's Temple was a CIA**

**experiment in group mind control gone badly. Mass quantities of various psychiatric drugs were discovered at Jonestown after the event. Psychiatrists *were* involved.**

Apparently "scientists" wanted to ascertain what people could be made to believe, and more importantly, what they could be manipulated into *doing* in the "name of" some religious creed or idea. The wanted to "study" by direct experimentation under controlled conditions, using the scientific method, the relationship of belief, conviction, and worship to actions, to the point of committing murder and suicide. Who knows where else and in what other situations they have done similar things? Be sure though, they have done it. That is the nature of "science" when applied to people and societies. Test-test-test and forget about one's conscience, decency and morality.

Again, to "learn" they had to "experiment". Realize this experimentation along these lines can only be highly oppressive and degrading to the victims. It serves no honest or decent useful purpose. It is another example of a crime against humanity, but hidden again behind deluded notions of "science", "the country's best interests" and "gaining knowledge". The real sick thing is that it makes perfect sense to those perpetrating these horrendous abuses. They don't think they are doing anything wrong, and ironically, some of them feel they are the most "dedicated", "honest" and "patriotic" folks compared to the rest of us. They "sacrifice a few to benefit the many, because it's the nature of war . . .".

They are severely deluded, and cause incredible harm to people and society.

Human history is primarily a comedy of errors. It is only one series of possibilities, stretched out over time and space, out of an infinite possible variety of alternatives. These "scientists" examine one small aspect of Man's history or culture, take it to be "the way things are", call the subject anthropology, and experiment along a similar path in an attempt to "understand" and "control". They never quite understand that what Man has been in the past too often has been largely due to oppression, ignorance (lack of education), deception (mis-education) and the abusive control of past kings, dictators, and Churches. Man has *never* been allowed to exist in an empowering environment that acknowledges and encourages all the good about him. That is equally true today. For "social science" to study and investigate these past instances of social circumstances with the idea of actually learning anything useful about human beings is absurd. It's dull people conducting equally dull studies. These people are largely morons despite all their complex studies and assertions.

They make another major error in theory and practice. The modern views of "social science" too often include the notion that "societies" and "groups" are actual organisms or entities with a life and existence of their own. Some asinine theorists (i.e. Hegel, Karl Marx, and John Dewey) even assert that the "social entity" is MORE important and has more validity than the individuals! Therefore they try to envision and create various social structures to bring about new, "better", and alternate conditions. They talk about the "ills of society", "social decay", "the State", "social tension", and "social harmony" as if these were real things. There is *no* "social" organism. There is *no* "organic whole of all life". These are concepts, abstractions, and ideas that exist ONLY in someone's head. They have no real basis in observable fact outside of the ideas certain men hold about them. And placing these concepts in positions of importance senior to the life of individual human beings is ludicrous and always results in harm to various members of the civilization involved.

The only *actual thing* is a human being, a unique individual mind, a person. All else is pretty much conceptions and ideas in his and others' minds. Any society, group or civilization is ONLY the sum total of all the individual people comprising it. What makes any society, group or civilization what it is involves only the *sum total* of all the notions, ideas, beliefs, values, decisions, responsibility, self-determinism, goals, and actions of the individual people involved. If anyone seriously wants to make a better society, civilization or world, the *only* correct and successful approach is to *first make better people*. There is no other way to do it. Strangely, no one even considers this approach today. Possibly the idea is too "simple" for the overly complex intellectuals of today. They would rather spend endless energy and time fabricating complex laws, legislation and social mandates, in their perverted attempts to "coerce" or "enable" Man to "evolve" and behave "appropriately". These modern politicians, social theorists and group psychologists are dolts. They spend all their time trying to come up with the "ideal social system", while continually ignoring the only thing that will ever bring about any real lasting improvement, the betterment and empowerment of the minds of individual men and women.  And that they don't deal with at all.


**Example #3:**

Another example is electric shock treatments.

The story of electric shock began in 1938, when Italian psychiatrist Ugo Cerletti visited a Rome slaughterhouse to see what could be learned from the method that was employed to butcher hogs. In Cerletti's own words,

"As soon as the hogs were clamped by the [electric] tongs, they fell unconscious, stiffened, and then after a few seconds they were shaken by convulsions. During this period of unconsciousness (epileptic coma), the butcher stabbed and bled the animals without difficulty....

"At this point I felt we could venture to experiment on man, and I instructed my assistants to be on the alert for the selection of a suitable subject."

Cerletti's first victim was provided by the local police - a man described by Cerletti as "lucid and well-oriented." After surviving the first blast without losing consciousness, the victim overheard Cerletti discussing a second application with a higher voltage. He begged Cerletti, "Non una seconda! Mortifierel" ("Not another one; it will kill me!").

Ignoring the objections of his assistants, Cerletti increased the voltage and duration and fired again. With the "successful" electrically induced convulsion of his victim, Ugo Cerletti brought about the application of hog-slaughtering skills to humans, creating one of the most brutal techniques of psychiatry.

At no point had anyone ever observed a human being benefiting, improving, becoming happier, or expanding in responsibility from an electric shock. What depraved stream of logic determines that submitting a human being to a hog-slaughtering technique is "therapeutic" or "helpful"?

But this is natural and business as usual for psychiatrists.

This is another example of "scientists" experimenting on human beings in an attempt to "learn" something, and to control. There has never been any basis in "science" for electric shock treatments. Yes, sure it changes people, but smashing them in the head with a baseball bat would also change them. Sticking bamboo shoots under their fingernails would surely change them.

**Psychiatrists and scientists have come up with many theories to "explain" how ECT "helps cure mental illness", but these are nothing more than fairy tales. And while reading a Grimm fairy tale hurts nobody, the modern fairy tales of the psychiatrists and psychologists are not so innocuous. Electric shock and other psychiatric methods cause severe harm while parading as "modern science", "cures" and "therapy".**

Human beings respond and react to force, whether that force be physical, chemical or electrical. *Never* is the application of any force helpful or empowering to the individual. Modern "science" is rooted in applying force or energy of some sort to some situation to bring about a change or new condition. This is fine and desirable in the pure physical sciences. Modern medicine, electronics, and various fields of engineering have made great strides in improving the physical condition of mankind. But force doesn't produce any decent or desirable results when applied to human beings. The result is *always* confusion, degradation, loss of personal responsibility, and chaos.

What works with people is appealing to understanding, communication, and interacting with the functions of the mind of the person. The approach of the modern psychiatrist, psychologist and social scientist is to apply the same notions of the physical sciences to the realm of Man, his mind and society. It doesn't "work". It will *never* "work". The only result will always be harm, failure, deterioration and the collapse of individuals and society. Take a look around. What Man lacks more than anything is an *understanding and science of his own mind*.

The successful "science" of physical matter and energy involves applying differing types of forces to bring about new conditions in controlled situations. It works in the realm of physical matter and energy. It does not work in the realm of human beings, human minds, and societies. The application of force to individual minds and societies has no possible positive rendition. Freedom, responsibility, self-determinism, morality and decency are incompatible with force, and therefore with any attempt at a scientific "solution" to Man and his societies. It simply can't and won't ever get anywhere decent or desirable for the people as a whole. Communism was an attempt at a "scientific" study and application to human beings and society. It depended almost completely on force, and obviously failed miserably, as it only could. Force, and therefore "science", is unworkable with people.

For "science" to work with human beings and societies, it must drastically alter its approach. There is nothing wrong with "science". In fact it is wonderful if used correctly. There is everything wrong with the manner in which purported "science" currently views and attempts to deal with human beings. The "scientific method" *is* extremely useful, but that isn't what is used in the subjects of psychology, psychiatry and the "social sciences". These fields have attached themselves to the concept of "science" in an attempt to gain legitimacy while actually promoting bias, opinion, and false notions about Man and his mind under a facade of "research" and "objective science".

**First, Man's mind is NOT matter or energy, The brain that houses the mind is matter and the chemical reactions in the brain are energy but the mind is best described as spirit and the energy thereof is from God to man. It doesn't function as if it is made of matter or energy, and cannot be "solved" by treating it as such. All attempts to do so will result in ultra-**

controlled, totalitarian systems with the individual oppressed.

Second, the "mind" of Man and all it is must be recognized as the *primary* aspect of value and importance with Man and his societies.

"Science" has never examined, with an aim to "solve" and "improve", *the mind of Man.*

What is it?
How does it work?
What are its functions?
What are its problems?
How can it be bettered?

It *has* been investigated, when considered at all, primarily from a viewpoint of how to *control* it. But modern psychiatry and psychology have largely abandoned all notions of a mind and instead concentrate on biochemistry, behavior, environmental factors (i.e. stimulus-response), and genetics. This will lead nowhere.

**Man is primarily a *mind*. A mind is aware, experiences, thinks, chooses, determines, imagines, conceives, considers, believes, conceptualizes, places attention, intends, sets goals, exerts discipline, adheres to accepted codes of conduct (morality) and can act responsibly according to self-determined decisions and agreements. THESE things need to be seriously acknowledged, investigated, studied, tested, and understood with an aim towards *empowering the individual*. The scientific method *could* be applied to these aspects of the human mind but never has been.**

**There is no extant subject dealing with these things anywhere within the traditional confines of modern education and thought. The aim of *control* would be one of "self-control", the control of one's *own* mind in all its aspects.**

One problem here is that for all practical purposes the mind and all its functions and contents are invisible. A thought can't be measured. An emotion can't be placed in a test tube. Imagination can't be weighed. A goal can't be quantified. A human intention can't be objectively viewed and examined with statistical analysis. Feelings of love, hate, anger or enthusiasm cannot be detected outside of the behaviors associated with them.

It's also difficult to know whether people undergoing "mental" experiments are doing what they say they are doing with their minds. This has been a real major stumbling block for the modern "scientist" familiar only with dealing with visible, tangible and physical things. The "things" of the mind are *not* visible or detectable in the same way as any other object of observation in the entire physical universe. Simply, the mind is of an entirely different nature and adheres to different laws. Anyone honestly observing their own mind will come to this same conclusion, and nobody else can ever do this for you. You are the only one who experiences your mind *as your mind* in the way you experience it. You know your thoughts, feelings, ideas, hopes, and goals are real, yet these are completely invisible to everyone else, and *vice versa*. "Objective" science is impossible when dealing with a mind because it can't be observed *as it is* by anyone except the person whose mind it is. This doesn't make scientific examination impossible, but it does necessitate a different approach to addressing the subject. The scientific approach used in the physical sciences can't be easily transferred to the realm of the mind where everything about it is invisible to objective detection.

Early psychologists from Germany in the late 1800s, Wilhelm Wundt and his followers, decided, "since the human mind and inner states cannot be observed or measured directly, we will ignore them, not deal with them at all and only concern ourselves with behavior". And so it has been ever since. It's not that the mind doesn't exist; each of us knows it does from our own direct personal experience, but the entire approach of "modern science" with this subject has *ignored and denied the mind* as a factor of importance and object of study. Considering that every decent, great or noble thing originated as an idea in the mind of some man or woman should make it fairly obvious that discarding the mind of Man as part of the basic underlying philosophical bent of various modern "social sciences" cannot ever have positive results.

**There needs to be an honest scientific examination of the mind of Man with an aim towards understanding, solving and improving it in all its aspects. But it must be dealt with on its *own level*, within its *own context*, and addressing its *own functions*. Trying to understand it and what it does from a framework of physical matter and energy is useless. As an example take the conservation of energy theory. This states that no matter or energy can be created newly, but**

only its form can be altered. **This is not true at all in the realm of mind. Man's imagination is constantly creating newly out of nothing....symphonies, plays, books, inventions, and so on. The functions of Man's mind are radically different than anything else observable "out there" in the material universe.**

What is attention?
How can it be strengthened, concentrated, directed, intensified, or reduced at will?
What drills are necessary to assist a person to become aware of and control their own attention?
What is the nature of concentration?
Can it be improved?
How so?
What exercises or drills lead to bettered concentration?
What is imagination?
What different types of imagination are there?
Can it be improved?
How?
What are goals?
How do they relate to reality, intention and determination?
Can intention and determination be increased?
How much?
How so?

This list of questions can easily get quite long. The mind is a completely unexamined and uncharted area requiring extensive investigation. The only way to effectively improve qualities of a mind is with "mental" techniques. Such techniques are strangely missing in the current fields related to the mind.

Many supposed "mental illnesses" such as depression, anxiety and compulsions are nothing more than a severe inability of the person to control and direct their own attention. This is not said to minimize the seriousness of the condition to the person who "suffers" from these things or to suggest they aren't real. They are real, but they don't exist as "illnesses" or "diseases". They *are* conditions, but are not adequately addressed and handled by a medical or biological approach. They are definitely NOT "physical illnesses". If a person truly learned how and was able to control where they allowed their own attention to fall, whether on external things and situations, or upon internal ideas, feelings or sensations, the power of these supposed "mental illnesses" would greatly decrease.

The only real "mental illness" in the world today is modern Man's almost complete lack of any understanding about his own mind, how to deal with it, and how to learn to gain control over it and everything it is capable of doing for and to him. Ultimately it *is* a matter of *control*, but of *self-control*, over that immense universe of thought we each possess, seemingly, though not necessarily, a few inches behind our foreheads.

**The modern approaches of psychiatry and psychology don't assume self-control is possible because they don't even consider your mind exists. To many of them the mind is nothing but an accidental by-product of chemical reactions in a brain, and an annoying by-product at that. It seems they would be**

**happiest if it didn't exist at all, and many of them are trying to bring such a view about.**

The mind *exists*. It *is* invisible. It does things that no matter or energy anywhere in the entire universe does. It's aware, it conceptualizes, it sets goals, it establishes values, it chooses, it intends, it appreciates, it admires, and it initiates action (to mention only a few). No example of matter or energy located anywhere in space or time, which is the subject of the physical sciences, does what a mind does. Someday some of these brilliant "scientists" may finally notice this and change their approach to the subject.

**A mind and all it does is *not* similar in nature to any of the objects of physical reality that a mind perceives and is aware of. So why treat it as if it is similar? This is simply a huge error of viewpoint on the subject. It is a basic assumption taken by the majority of people, which is just plain incorrect.**

Also, the purpose of such a scientific investigation cannot be to manipulate, control, force or dictate belief, thought, ideas or actions against the will of the person. People need to be educated into the discoveries of a scientific examination of the mind, and each individual placed in *control of their own mind* with tools to understand and improve their own mind. Too often others decide what the beliefs, attitudes and behaviors should be. This must stop or this civilization will continue to decline and fail.

The current "scientific" approach to Man and his mind is wrong, 180 degrees wrong in the opposite direction of what could and would help individual people and also thereby, their societies, which are nothing more than groups of *individual people*. There will never be success viewing and treating Man as only so much matter, energy, chemicals, atoms and electrical reactions.

This is why psychiatry can only fail. It views and treats Man as matter and energy, and their only "solution" is force, because force is the only "solution" in the realm of matter and energy. You can't get a rock to move by appealing to its "understanding". It moves only by brute force. You *can* get a person to move by appealing to "understanding". "Understanding" is one of these "mind qualities". People *aren't* rocks, *shouldn't* be treated as such, but this is functionally the view and approach taken by psychiatry, which *does* depend completely upon *force*; physical force by involuntary commitment, restraints, deprogramming techniques, lobotomy, and straight jackets, electrical force by electric shock treatments, chemical force by powerful, brain-altering and mind-altering psychotropic drugs.

At no point does the "modern scientific" approach consider, acknowledge, address or better *any human mind* on the level of and within the context of the functions of a human mind. In fact, modern psychiatry flat-out *denies* the existence of a "mind". This basic philosophical error of psychiatry in understanding and "treating" Man, *the denial of the human mind*, makes any attempts to improve Man doomed to fail within the context of their grossly flawed theories and methods.

Of course, psychiatry's goal has never been to "help", empower or bring about increased happiness, success, self-determinism or responsibility in any individual human being. Their goal has always only been about controlling behavior, behavior that others find objectionable or inconvenient. This explains why governments and intelligence agencies have worked with and funded psychiatry and modern psychology for so many years. Their goal is often also control of the thoughts, beliefs and actions of the people. Sadly, this is as true for American "democracy" as it is for any totalitarian regime such as communist China or a South American dictatorship. The common denominator of them all is control, and psychiatry and modern psychology supply them with important "tools" to achieve their aims. If the theories and methods of modern psychology and psychiatry led to individual personal expansion, happiness, mental stability, certainty, knowledge, freedom, responsibility, awareness and self-determined moral action, then no totalitarian government would ever have supported them. But then psychiatry and modern psychology *don't* lead to these things and governments *do* very much support them.

## I Have a Special Gift for My Readers

I appreciate my readers for without them I am just another author attempting to make a difference. If my book has made a favorable impression please leave me an honest review.    Thank you in advance for you participation.

My readers and I have in common a passion for the written word as well as the desire to learn and grow from books.

My special offer to you is a massive ebook library that I have compiled over the years. It contains hundreds of fiction and non-fiction ebooks in Adobe Acrobat PDF format as well as the Greek classics and old literary classics too.

In fact, this library is so massive to completely download the entire library will require over 5 GBs open on your desktop.

Use the link below and scan all of the ebooks in the library. You can select the ebooks you want individually or download the entire library.

The link below does not expire after a given time period so you are free to return for more books rather than clog your desktop. And feel free to give the link to your friends who enjoy reading too.

I thank you for reading my book and hope if you are pleased that you will leave me an honest review so that I can improve my work and or write books that appeal to your interests.

Okay, here is the link…

http://tinyurl.com/special-readers-promo

PS: If you wish to reach me personally for any reason you may simply write to mailto:support@epubwealth.com.

I answer all of my emails so rest assured I will respond.

## Meet the Author

Dr. Harry Jay is Director of Research for AppliedMindSciences.com, a mental health and mind research group of Applied Web Info, and is the author of over 100 books and research papers as a behavioral scientist.

In his 32-year career, Dr. Harry Jay has contributed many new mental health treatment treatments and protocols using some of the new advances he has discovered in Energy Psychology.

He specializes in addictions of all kinds, sexual abuse, child predation and gender relationships.

He is also a board member to ePubWealth.com and serves on the science committee assisting non-fiction science writers in book publishing and promotion.

As a leading behavioral scientist, he provides profiling services to the company's ForensicsNation.com unit as well as criminal psychology research to aid in identifying and apprehending child predators and cyber-criminals of all kinds.

He resides in Southern Utah and enjoys the outdoors, fishing and photography.

**Visit some of his websites**

http://www.AddMeInNow.com
http://www.AppliedMindSciences.com
http://www.BookbuilderPLUS.com
http://www.BookJumping.com
http://www.EmailNations.com
http://www.EmbarrassingProblemsFix.com
http://www.ePubWealth.com
http://www.ForensicsNation.com
http://www.ForensicsNationStore.com
http://www.FreebiesNation.com
http://www.HealthFitnessWellnessNation.com
http://www.Neternatives.com
http://www.PrivacyNations.com
http://www.RetireWithoutMoney.org
http://www.SurvivalNations.com
http://www.TheBentonKitchen.com
http://www.Theolegions.org
http://www.VideoBookbuilder.com

www.ingramcontent.com/pod-product-compliance
Lightning Source LLC
Chambersburg PA
CBHW070438290526
45791CB00005B/2028

*9 7 8 1 4 9 5 3 4 9 9 3 5 *